Tidal Waves of Love

Volume 1

By

Hope Moore

Table of Contents

Dedication

I dedicate this book to all the beautiful souls, that struggle with loving themselves.

Acknowledgments

To Carlos, my best friend. Thank you for loving me through every stage.

To my grandparents, thank you for instilling in me a love for reading and writing at a young age.

To the love of my life, thank you for showing me I'm worthy of love. Thank you for pushing me to keep going.

To my sisters, thank you for supporting me.

To my parents, thank you for all your love.

To my fans, thank you for being the reason I write. Thank you for being my motivation and so much more.

To my friends, thank you for all your kind words and support.

I love you all.

The

First

Wave.

Tidal Waves of Love

Standing in front of the lucid blue ocean.
I allowed my petals of hurting to fall.
One by one they floated out to sea.
Leaving me with just a stem,
And thorns slightly cutting my hands.
So, I followed behind them.
Diving into the vast tidal waves.
Without any need to stay afloat.
Because they would teach me,
Everything I needed to know.
Stripping away my self-doubts,
And forcing me to push love into myself.
I called them *Tidal Waves of Love*.

There I sat, just me at peace.
Listening to the sound of raindrops.
Softly falling onto my windowpane.
Sipping a warm cup of herbal tea.
Enjoying the company of myself.
Cherishing the sound of the heavy rain.
The clink of my yellow ceramic spoon.
Slowly tracing the interior of my mug.
And the silence in between,
Every I love you spoken within me.

Looking into a mirror,
Staring back at me is me.
As I look into my tired eyes,
I want to fall in love with the view.
Embracing myself endlessly,
Like I have once before.

~I want to *try again*.

Glow

I dug deep into the realms of my beliefs,
To grab a handful of self-love.
That was hiding deep inside of me,
From the judgment of prying eyes.
I pulled them up to the surface,
And all I whispered was, "Go."
They took off into a full-on *glow*,
Letting no soul lock them up again.

I lived with treasured bruises.
Thick and purple-hued.
On the surface of my heart.
From every punch I threw,
Straight from my mouth.
That traveled to my soul.
And whispered to my body.
That it wasn't *good enough.*

Storms and Thoughts

When the storm comes,
I run through puddles into hiding.
Underneath an umbrella of self-scrutiny.
While attempting to flee from the thoughts,
That crash like thunder into my mind.
Instead of soaking in the rain,
That will transform me into a sunflower.
Allowing me to see storms and thoughts,
As necessities needed for me to evolve.

It's Okay

I kissed all the hate that lived in me.
Letting it know it was okay to love.
There's power in being vulnerable.
To be fragile and resilient too,
Like Viola's at the start of Autumn.
It's okay to let love fiercely flood my mind.
Secret doors to new worlds are unlocked,
Once my chains of coldness dissolve.

Fueled

You've been fused and fueled.
By the fumes of self-hatred.
Light the match,
That will ignite the flames.
Of love, that your soul has craved.
Let the heat course through your body.
Burning every inch of self-negativity.
That you cast upon yourself.
Unique souls like yours,
Deserve to be cherished and preserved.
Like antique paintings from centuries ago.

My Savior

My body is my savior.
Shielding me from intruders of the soul.
A glove that gives me warmth,
And embraces every part of me.
Getting me through each day.
Filling my lungs with unconditional love.
Singing me to sleep with lullabies.
That are infused with reasons,
On why we are beautiful as one.

Love Leaks

Like rare fish swimming in the ocean,
I dived into the tidal waves of my body.
To swim within them freely,
Without any worry of predators below me.
Causing a ripple effect of change within my sea.
Letting love leak into every part of my being.

All the wrong feelings overwhelmed my happiness.
They were drenched in a liquid paste full of hate.
But I'm grateful for all the wrong things.
They allowed me to be open and bloom.
Like a rose during the warm-clean air of spring.
Allowing all the right things to enter my world.

You do not need validation for your size,
From the tainted view of another's eyes.
Their approval holds no weight,
To the magic that thrives in self-acceptance.

YOU

I thought life was about finding love.
Lover after lover, I felt incomplete.
Like a band looking for a lead singer,
But constantly finding the wrong voice.
It took years of searching,
Through confusing forests and valleys.
Down roads and highways named after my life.
Leading me to an abandoned billboard.
That had the word "YOU" printed in bold.
Big enough for the world to see.
That "YOU" was representing me.
Then I realized to love, I must love myself.
To connect with a lover, I need to connect with myself.
To spread kindness into the world,
I need to be kind to every part of myself.

House Fire

You say you're a house fire.
Tell me,
Who poured gasoline into your soul?
Who lit the match that broke you?
Allowing you to sink into ashes.
Feeling lifeless and dead inside.
Sending your love into flames.
Tell me,
Who said to stop loving yourself?
You may be damaged and in need of repair.
But your bones are antique structures.
You deserve to be appraised at the highest price.
Loved beyond the sky we see above.
You say you're a house fire.
Grab a hose filled with water,
And shower yourself back into self-love.

Never apologize,
For knocking down used doors.
That stayed tightly sealed in hatred.
For everything that makes you.
Old doors and screws must fall,
If you want to become a better you.

Strong

Once you start to love yourself,
Your mind won't feel clouded.
You won't find a need to question,
Those who see beauty in you.
People who try to love you,
And water you with your magic.
Because of the love you've bathed in,
Your vision will be vivid and clear.
Like fog, disappearing to reveal a sunrise.
You'll finally see what we feel.
To feel the love of others,
Overwhelm you in this realm.
You must love yourself, strongly.
Stronger than rip tides.
That crash into fragile wooden docks,
Already hidden below the surface of the sea.

Self-love is a whisper.
In a world that only shouts,
Screaming out for hatred.
But listen closely for the whisper.
I promise it's there.
It's there.

Only Once

He told me we could get married.
But only once my ring size shrank.
Dwindling to a single-digit number,
Smaller than his massive shoe size.
Only once the smell of carbs and fats,
No longer left me salivating with no control.
Only once my body could bend and squeeze,
Into size four dresses I was never able to fit.
Only once his eyes scream "yes she's the model."
The one you've been searching for endlessly.
You can marry her now; the rest is history.

Like the vast sky and galaxies,
Beyond the ability of our reach.
Love, you are untouchable.

Deserve

You think you're too hard to love,
Because they tend to leave you.
Quicker than the wind in a gust,
Blowing you north to south.
Like a paper ball rolling hundreds of miles,
Down steep inclines and rough concrete.
But until you halt at a yellow light.
Faced with the choice of tumbling down,
Or flying up with love for who you are.
No one will stay until you see what you deserve.

Love glitters on my skin.
Shining radiant gold hues,
That bounce of the eyes of a few.
Dancing on the tip of my tongue.
As I speak words of incredible truth.
Traveling through my mind,
Planting seeds of affection inside.
So I can one day describe,
And tell a captivating tale.
Of how love was the love of my life.

Time

I was time's fool.
Allowing it to pass me.
Without a need to hide,
Or deny the things inside.
As it silently stole my jewels.
Like the love, I lost for myself,
That gradually died over time.
Good habits for my soul,
Like planting and picking flowers.
For myself, not anyone else.
Time passed, my life was passing,
And I never even noticed.

I learned to fill my cup,
Before pouring into others.
How can I love another?
With an inability to love me.

The Art of Your Stature

Fall in love with your stature.
Whether your ribs may be exposed,
Or your love handles dip into your hips.
You were designed as one of a kind.
Like a piece of art by Michelangelo.
You cannot be replicated.
Your worth cannot be stolen.
Your stature is nothing but art.

Perfect

It's not about being perfect.
It's about loving every unique code within.
The beautiful contents that run in your DNA.
It's about acceptance and embracing.
Hugging every part of your soul that is pained.
Nourishing your spirit with soulful words.
It was never about being perfect.
Because we are all imperfect,
Searching for the key that unlocks this perfection.
But there is no key to this imaginary door.
We are all perfect in the eyes of the right person.
We are all perfect when we look in the mirror,
And we fall in love with the reflection.
We are all perfect when we embrace our imperfections.

Your body has hearing greater than bats.
Be careful what you speak within your mind.
As she can hear your words, and they are piercing.
Speak waves of love only, so she knows you care.

Tainted Image

My condolences to my old and lost feelings.
That don't deserve to be mourned.
I set them free so I could believe.
Believe that I deserved to be loved,
To be cherished and admired.
Without a tainted image reflecting onto me.

Gold

You tumbled out of alignment with your worth.
Falling into perfect alignment with your wounds.
To dig yourself out of the trap of your hurt,
You must realize your worth surpasses tons of gold.
The beauty of your spirit is timeless,
And your soul has the highest price tag.

~You are gold.

Plant your heart with the soil of confidence.
Become the gardener of your soul.
Watering yourself with self-love,
Blooming into the rose you always were.

Lost Love

I lost my love for myself,
But I found it again.
Within every hidden structure,
Of my beauty inside and out.
I found love between each stretch mark.
Every bump on my face held the key to my soul.
Acceptance for my body and my sensitive mind,
Led to love beyond my comprehension.
Unlocking mountains of love for every part of me.
That never got to see the rays of the sun and its light.
The parts that never got nurtured and watered.
They will flourish now,
My love will make sure of it.

Justified Insecurities

I justified my insecurities too often.
I took the opinions of others too harshly.
I convinced myself it was my problem.
Slowly picking myself apart.
Finding new problems with my face,
Or my legs, and little things like my clothes.
But the conflict never lived within me.
It was thriving in a world that didn't want me.

Be careful and tread lightly,
On the track of self-criticism.
Powder and sugar look the same.
Don't mistake criticism for critiquing.

Show up

I stood by the clock.
Watching it fiercely,
As it ticked and it moved.
Waiting for my confidence,
To return to its home in me.
So I could show up.
Turning the heads of many,
And causing envious eye rolls.
Somehow, she never returned.
And I had to show up anyway.
With a pen I wrote my spoken vows,
That I would never wait again.
Confidence or not, I'll show up.

I shed away my extra layers.
Allowing my skin to marinate in the sun.
Seeping through the cracked walls,
And the tipping steps to my heart.
I became my only hero, for once.
Unpacking all the self-doubt I buried.
To burn it under the eyes of the sun.

Fire Balloon

When I light a match to my soul,
I ignite like a fire balloon.
Floating into the air,
With love sprinkling behind me.
Because I was made from love.
A love that I fed my spirit,
So I could spread that love.
Floating in my fire balloon,
Searching for someone, anyone,
That may need this love next.

Barbie

None of it makes sense,
Sometimes we break ourselves.
Like the way we dismantled barbie dolls.
When we were young and wanted to play.
We break things we love,
Even if that thing is us.
Until we build ourselves back up.
Like putting new clothes onto our barbie,
Brushing her hair and grabbing her purse.
Taking care of her once again.

Under the enticing moonlit sky,
Daydream amongst lavender clouds.
Float gracefully into a soothing trance.
Escaping into a world full of you.

Open

As the last leaf in the fall fell to the ground,
I knew I had to let the hate go tonight.
As the sunset vanished into an indigo night sky,
I let my insecurities disappear into the stars.
I wrapped my thoughts in the thick clouds,
So they could grow soft and open.
Creating love within every piece of the sky.

I wrote a love letter to myself.
I sealed it with a kiss,
And tucked it under my pillow.
Next time I'm resting in bed,
And I get lonely, or I feel worthless.
I'll open it and reassure myself,
That all these thoughts are false.
I am loved, I have worth,
And I'm never alone.
I have the best lover,
Living within my body.

Surrounded

Surround yourself with everything that ignites your soul.
The people and places that inspire you to grow.
To be a wiser, kinder, healthier, loving human being.
The energy you allow to infiltrate your bubble,
Will slowly affect how beautifully you evolve.
Make sure the energy is right before allowing it in tight.

Don't float in between the idea of change.
The person you envision yourself being,
Wake up with the sun and be that version of you.
Stay up during the wee hours talking to the moon.
Manifesting the evolution of your soul.

Make It Happen

Only a goddess can make it happen.
While holding nothing but fine sand,
That slips through thin cracks easily.
Turning a drop of water into oceans.
Healing wounds made of glass,
By the grace of your touch.
Only a goddess can have nothing,
And transform it into jewels and gold.
Melting them down into magic,
Used to power your being.
Allowing the world to go round.
Because only a goddess like you,
Can make anything happen.

Your Table

You've been begging for a seat.
When you have all the tools to build a table.
Grab some Mahogany wood and gold screws.
Make your seat out of white oak and diamonds.
Invite only the finest to sit at your table with you.

Intertwine

My dislike for my body felt shady,
Like emotional downpour disguised as drizzles.
That flooded whole cities made of love,
And destructed countries full of acceptance.
Crashing into towns that lived in my veins.
Granting me with the wisdom I needed,
To remove the fog-filled cloud from my eyes.
Allowing me to intertwine into a loop of love.
Falling into a divine marriage with my body.

Bloom

The season has arrived.
Stop allowing dead weeds to grow.
Sprouting harmfully into your soul.
Blocking you from your growth.
Pull them up from their roots,
And watch as you transform and bloom.

Self-love Journey

My self-love journey was a chase.
Running faster than the speed of light,
Like I was attempting to win an Olympic race.
As I got close enough to touch it,
It'd speed up, going faster than before.
Leaving my hands in a tight grip that missed.
It wasn't until I slowed down like a snail,
Waiting for it to follow my lead and let us be.
Allowing me to grab it in a loving embrace.

I decided to stop being frightened.
By the road I was stuck on for so long.
Instead of letting fear consume me,
I became charged and inspired to go.
Speeding down that highway going 95 mph.
Racing towards the woman I was meant to be.

For My Body and Soul

Please forgive me.
For neglecting you,
Starving you of love.
Forgive me.
For the piercing words,
That I've coldly spoken to you.
Forgive me.
For not making you my only priority.
Pushing you to the back of the line.
Letting myself trample and destroy you.
Forgive me for not seeing your beauty.
When you've always reflected me.

My inability to love myself was a glass garden.
Cutting my fingertips with every pick of a flower.
Forcing me to approach myself with caution.
Never allowing too much love to seep or slip with ease.
Protecting my heart from the fragile idea of maybes.
Tiptoeing around the possibilities of our love.

<u>Shine</u>

Midnight memories strike my mind.
Reminding me of the times you were mine.
Before I let the world break you down,
Tossing you to the ground, never to feel love again.
Midnight memories strike my mind.
To tell me I must strive to make this right.
Uniting us as one, once again as we belong.
What is my mind and soul without your glow?
I let them steal your shine, but I promise to return it.

I uncovered my beauty that was there all along.
Like shoveled snow revealing earthy grass.

Energy

I embraced the crinkles and bags,
That wrapped around my sapphire eyes.
Recognizing that I survived,
While being exhausted.
I manifested countless dreams,
While feeling weak and powerless.
My feet may be tired,
But the love for myself is activated.
With nothing but genuine energy.

Watered Fears

I kept watering my fears,
Until I was left dry and brittle.
I never allowed myself to bloom.
I never encouraged my fears,
To bloom into actions or dreams.
To sprout into a love,
That I could never try to erase.
Instead, I fed my fire of fear.
Bottling them up until I shattered.
Searching for a source of water,
To feed on and devour my soul.
Consuming me back into my life.

You Aren't Alone

As I walk the streets stranded,
With no compass ticking towards the north.
My feet step to the beat of your scent.
Searching for your eyes, city to city,
Hoping to find you somewhere in the shadows.
In old bookstores, between the shelves.
Where books are unraveling at their bindings.
In local coffee shops, in tucked-away corners,
Where lost souls come to think and be unseen.
If it starts to pour waterfalls of rain onto this city,
I'll search coast to coast, to find you in the sun.
On a vast beach with your toes sinking,
Quickly sinking lower and lower like quicksand.
I'll be there to take you by both of your arms,
Pulling you from the grasp of the floor.
Letting you know that you don't have to run,
I will love you; you aren't alone anymore.

I want rose petal confetti,
For all of us who found self-love.
After being told we weren't worth it.
After climbing to the peak of mountains,
To scream out our testimonies from the top.

Safe Havens

I built a road in the wee hours of the night,
Hoping I'd find love by morning light.
But it only led me to a deserted highway,
Going to a place love wasn't, nowhere.
Stopping along the road, I noticed a field.
Crowded with flowers, water, and life.
I discovered something new.
Even the most isolated places,
Hold hidden safe havens.

I dipped my heart in an everlasting embrace.
Assuring her that she'd feel love forever.
If she beats with me as one.
And trusts that I can lead us to better places.
To eternal happiness, that we never had.

Resides

Come search for the secrets within my eyes.
I've seen tragedies you could never visualize.
Borrow my ears to hear the painful words.
That has pierced my ears all the days of my life.
Let me take off my sneakers and lend them to you.
So you can feel the miles I run from hurting.
Skip through the passageways of my mind,
And I'll show you all the darkness that resides.

Brain Food

You enjoyed bread before your meal,
And a glass of fruit punch during.
When did you switch to salad?
With iced water and a small slice of lemon.
Was it your choice to make this change?
Or did this vast world coerce you?
Into the belief that meals should always be light.
Due to your love handles,
The extra weight and the shape of your thighs.
They shouldn't contain more than 300 calories.
And your stomach should be left hungry.
But this was never true love listen to me,
You can eat wiser, but you don't need to feel weak.
Stumbling down walkways with a foggy mind.
Enjoy your brain food so you can be the best you.

This partnership with myself,
Is a timeless and delicate love.
So, I treat it with caution.
Slowly picking its fragile petals,
So the whole rose doesn't come undone.

Beautiful Girl

Can you remind me what it feels like?
To believe that I was born beautiful.
The days where I would never dare,
To compare myself to another woman.
When I felt like I was uniquely glamorous.
Before magazines, movies, and men,
Redefined the definition of a beautiful girl.

Blooming

Some things shatter, some things bloom.
I wonder which path I will choose.
Shattering and breaking is all I've ever known.
I want to gather the strength to bloom too.
As my petals grow, they retreat into their stems.
Scared of being destroyed, as they surface.
By the hate that lingers throughout my life.
When they come back, brave, and vibrant.
I will fight for them, embracing them finally.
Because blooming is what I always deserved.
Loving myself is the only way out.

The sunrise lived within my eyes.
Every sunset took residence in my heart.
All the beautiful things engulfed my spirit.

Wishes

I should have talked to myself more.
Assuring my spirit that I heard her.
Instead of turning off the sound of her voice.
I should have asked her how she was feeling.
Every time I spoke down on this shared body.
Making her feel like we were weeds,
In the middle of a vast field of flowers.
I should have talked to myself more.
Manifesting everything I could not do.
Sending her wishes to the moon and stars.
I should have known that I had the entire universe,
Resting in between the four walls of my room.

Love

Love is never wasted,
It transforms into you.
Gifting you so much love.
You become love.
You are the sweetest love.

I stepped outside into a world of ideas,
The air brimming with possibilities,
And the sun yelling "You can do anything."

To Those Who Lack Empathy

Am I too sensitive? Or are you unresponsive?
How does it feel to be cold?
Turning everything you touch,
Into ice that can never melt.
Am I too sensitive? Or do you just lack empathy?
Enabling you to not feel a thing.
Yes, I am sensitive, I feel things deeply.
So I internalize all your negative energies.
Halting that lack of empathy in your reach,
From seeping into this world.
Letting me brighten the days of others,
Like the sun gifting you it's rays.
My sensitivity ignites the flame,
A flame called sympathy.
Allowing me to turn regular words,
Into empowering speeches.
I encourage my sensitivity to keep growing.
Because she's the reason, that you just read this.

Saturated Bliss

Pumpkin scented bubble baths.
Cinnamon-soaked candles,
And love-drenched novels.
Saturated bliss.
Helping me nurture my spirit.
Today is a self-care day.

The Moon and Sunlight

I started to take care of my body.
Prescribing it to the moonlight.
Consuming a daily diet of sunlight.
And speaking words of dreams at night.
So by the time, the sun rises again.
I'll be ready to live unapologetically.
By the grace of the sun's healthiness,
And the healing contents of the moon.

This war is only temporary,
This pain riddled conflict.
That won't rest within me.
I hope for the day,
Fighting for power concludes.
The day love pours from my body,
Ready to grow and bloom.

<u>Softness</u>

Grab a handful of softness,
And place it upon your chest.
In alignment with your heart.
So it can melt like marshmallows,
Over a fire on a hot August day.
Seeping into your body,
Breaking down your walls.
So you can finally let love heal you.

New Mindset

Hidden secrets and betrayals,
Inflicted onto my soul and me.
How could I hurt my heart and mind?
With false beliefs of worthlessness,
And a lack of love that I always desired.
When the clock strikes twelve,
I'll let go of the hate that is no longer wanted.
To engulf my body in love, sealed and delivered.
From the depths of my heart,
That has finally been set free.
At the start of a new day and a new hour,
Welcomes the beginning of a new mindset.

I was trembling on thin ice.
Slowly stepping across,
Trying not to break my heart.
With icicle sharp words,
And over freezing thoughts.

Full

Sour to my soul, the hate lingered.
Placebo bitter sauces on my food.
To convince me not to eat.
Lines turning and swirling upon my body,
Drawing the reasons why hunger isn't real.
Toxic patterns embedded into my mind.
Now I'm up till the sunrise over the toilet,
Excreting everything that feels like an intruder.
But I'm done with these cycles of hate and lies.
By the time the moon rises, I will consume everything.
Ending the night with a full heart, body, and mind.

Hope Moore

I started to begin each day,
With hope dipped in honey.
That I would slowly stir into my tea.
Releasing nothing but optimism,
Into every living cell in my bloodstream.

No Bridge

A perfectly ruined thing,
This union of love.
Between me and my body.
I allowed people to wedge,
And cut the strings of our bond.
Leaving us with broken memories.
A damaged future full of dreams,
And no bridge to lead us back into love.

All The New

Silk winds brush my cheeks,
As I step outside into warmth.
Embracing the lightness in the air.
The daisies blooming in my garden,
And the reflection of the sun.
As it glistens in my copper fountain.
This spring, I will love this world.
But I'll love myself even more.
Because spring was made for all the new.
And what is newer than this love for me?

I wrapped my body in gold leaf.
So I'd glisten with every leak of light.
In every glance, I took passing a mirror.
Believing I was worth something after all.

Rest

As I laid my head down, ready to slip into dreams.
I let my head slowly sink into my satin pillowcase.
Attempting to sleep peacefully, but insomnia struck me.
Continuously tossing around for hours.
I felt like I was laying in someone else's bed.
As if my body was not mine to lay to rest.
I lacked adequate sleep within my home.
Until I became one with my body, appreciating it.
Filling it up with mountains of love and kindness.
Allowing it to finally rest under every night sky.

A soul's ingredients are doused in self-love.
Reach deep down inside for the missing parts.
That will complete the recipe needed.
Letting you bake into your sweetest self.

<u>Seek</u>

Search and seek sunshine.
For once you look towards the light,
There's no going back to the dark.
Let the sun soak into your skin,
Filling you up with body positivity.
Allowing waves of self-esteem,
To flood all negativity out of your body.
Use the warmth to power your soul.
Sprinkling you with the strength,
And mindset to overcome any and everything.

Relinquish Control

I must relinquish control,
If I want to feel whole.
I may have a broken heart,
But it's also a fresh start.
A new day has dawned.
One I have badly longed.
So I could start to love.
Gifted by the powers of above.
My higher self is always right.
So I tend to fight her with all my might.

Castle Ruins

I destroyed the only home I had.
I was joyful even when I was sullen.
But I knocked it down anyway,
With my bare hands and feet.
I kicked and clawed it to a crumble,
Brick by brick, I watched it fall.
As it came tumbling down,
My heart followed too.
Like a domino effect,
I was left with nothing but castle ruins.

Make love to yourself more.
Devour all positive things about yourself.
Lift your spirit with encouraging words.
Spend time gifting yourself items you desire.
Kiss your thoughts, showing them great affection.
Feed your soul all the ways to love itself.

The Rainbow

What's at the end of the rainbow?
Is gold sitting on its last legs?
Waiting for me to collect it,
And breathe meaning into its life.
Are dark clouds forming at the bottom?
Tricking me into a pit of darkness.
Is the rainbow I see in the sky real?
Or is it reflecting hues that they don't own?
Showing me everything I want to see.
Deceiving me to believe that I can be a rainbow.
Tall, free, and colorful again.
Looking down at myself from above,
Spreading love into my eyes.
That will infect the rest of my soul.

Your Wings

What happened to your wings?
The ones that took you to discreet skies.
Where you could sleep in the clouds,
Dreaming in a peaceful world.
Embracing your curves and how they sink.
Admiring your toes and their point.
The realm where you could feel flawless.
Without the voice of anyone else screaming,
"You're not."

Unrefined

Every night I had enchanted visions.
That would crash into my mind,
Like a pile-up truck collision.
Leaving me with desires to find.
And riddled with decisions.
Will I be left behind?
Switching and changing positions?
Until I unite my spirits, unrefined.

I used to drape my heart in blue,
Sinking into erratic thoughts.
Now, I wrap my heart in plush pinks.
Floating on top of healthy beliefs.

Faint Echoes

I heard the faint echoes of my voice.
Hiding between each sorrow in my heart.
I searched for the sound endlessly.
Jumping through the hoops of my mind.
Sliding down avalanches that festered within.
Attempting to turn the knob on every locked door.
Until I finally found and loved it into silence.

New Beginning

It smells like a new beginning,
As I skip into my garden to plant sunflowers.
A day where loving myself is an easy task.
I go for my morning jog because I deserve to.
Pouring streams of my favorite sugared creamer.
Into each of my cups of coffee because I can indulge.
Binging my new television series in bed,
Because I don't have to do *something* today.
I owe it to myself to do what I desire today,
Even if I desire to do *nothing*.

You can heal your wounds,
And watch your battle scars fade.
Without becoming a new you,
Tainted by the person who hurt you.

Fleeting Moment

Enjoy this fleeting moment.
You'll never get today back.
Cherish the way you feel.
Admire your beauty in this hour.
Nourish your heart with soulful words.
Give yourself ample amounts of love.
This moment and this minute can't be re-lived.
Be sure that you invested your time into love.

I told my body, "Tell me all the ways to love you."
She replied, "Stop listening to the opinions of others."

Defeat

I began to live life waiting.
Waiting for a taste of tomorrow.
A new day that would bring new feelings.
But hours, months, or years can't erase this.
This built-up self-hatred I have within.
Only I can conquer and defeat this battle.
Claiming my trophy labeled "self-love."

Fingers crossed that this arrow won't miss.
The one cupid attempts to shoot into my heart.
That will cast a spell on my mind.
Devouring my thoughts and feelings.
Pushing me into a divine love with myself.

Secluded

I fled to secluded shores,
So I could bathe in the ocean freely.
Without the view of prying eyes.
Wearing my favorite two-piece,
Feeling comfortable in my skin.
Embracing the tiger marks,
That run across my stomach.
Creating artwork down to my thighs.
As I ran into the calming waves,
I thanked them for accepting me.
The waves whispered, "They will too."

You do not have to overindulge,
To enjoy the food you like to eat.
It is okay to feel happy in your skin.
It is okay to enjoy meals you like.
At night when you lay your head to rest,
The world will not be there comforting you.
Your soul will and your body too.

The Scent of Acceptance

I left my skin feeling haunted.
Laced with fragile cracked bones.
Alongside tainted eyes and a broken heart.
But the scent of acceptance,
Always trailed close, right under my nose.
Sending me signs driven by gravity,
And every star in the sky, leading me home.
Screaming "This scent should be in your life."

<u>Bloom</u>

You must learn to be patient with the journey.
Bouquets of roses don't grow overnight.
Neither will you, so you must nurture yourself.
Water your soul from the deepest part of its roots.
And diligently watch as you bloom beautifully.
Into a field of roses infused with all your self-love.

I weathered the hurricane in my chest.
Breaking it down to a drizzle.
Slowly letting the clouds evaporate.
Giving the sun room to shine its light,
Into the darkest parts of my heart.

Flawed

My demons were flawed.
Corrupting me to morph into them.
Becoming one with my demons.
Rather than fighting them off,
Eliminating all their flaws.
Claiming control of my temple.

Cry

Crying is self-love too.
Find your place to cry.
Underneath your peeling wallpaper,
Peel away the layers of your hurt.
Lay in bed under your velvet blanket,
Let the warmth seep into your heart.
Release your burdens through each teardrop.
Crying was never a sign of weakness.
It's one of your greatest strengths.
Transforming all your traumas,
Into love that ripples like waves.

My heart is tipping over at its capacity.
Overflowing with limitless power.
I am glowing in the sparks of love.
Blasting out rays of colorful hues.
Like fireworks in the depths of my chest.
The greatest sight on a hot July night,
Is now alive within my body.

How did you feel about your body?
Before the world started to pry,
And suggest how you should feel?

The Good Days

These words and resurfacing thoughts are embedded.
Embedded into my brain like a battle is to a warrior.
This conviction of worthlessness still haunts me.
These chaotic brain patterns hinder my growth.
Memories of times when I spoke empty promises.
Because they were the only things, I could give myself.
Hoarding everything beautiful that lives within me.
But I will unlock this door to an everlasting paradise.
I won't allow the good days to become lost in the past.

Chaos

Chaos induced collapsing moments.
Stirred in between the walls of my mind.
Inflicting me with thoughts of disapproval.
Watching as I crumble from mountains to dust.
Left underneath the rubble, forced to save myself.

The Horizon

My happiness is over the horizon.
Making it hard for me to see it,
To admire its strength for surviving.
Through all the crushed dreams,
And harsh realities that live in me.
By the time the sun sets,
And the moon takes over for the night.
I'll be on top of the horizon.
Waiting to intertwine with my happiness.
Once again, living in its embrace forever.

My self-love was the lightning bolt.
That lit up my empty blue sky.
Allowing me to feel alive.
Striking down everything in my way.

Infinite

Do you believe in second chances?
I believe we are infinite.
Let me love you into starlight.
The shelter you seek within the orange skies.
Let our love sprout, just one more time.

I became the reason I smiled.
The only way I would feel love.
Transforming into the lover I desired.
Granting myself every single wish,
That fell onto the deaf ears of my past.

Growing

I used to feel destroyed,
By the challenges I'd go through.
Until I realized that I wasn't *going,*
I was *growing* through it all.

The

Wave

Of

Affirmations

Today will bring me serenity.
I will find joy in being me.
I will search for happiness.
I control the waves ahead of me.

I will remain authentic to myself.
I will reject all societal pressures.
I will not follow another's expectations.
I'm releasing what does not serve me.

I am no longer available for things that make me feel inferior.
I will no longer associate with people who think they are superior.

I deserve to breathe without concern.
Today I will relax and release my worries.
This day is just a chapter in my life.
Not my whole life wrapped into a novel.

Not everything I lose is a loss.
I must let things go to grow.

I will not judge myself by the thoughts of others.
Only my opinions hold weight and are valid.
I harness the power to shape my thoughts.
I am in control, I'm beautiful, and that is power.

I can only love others the way I love myself.
I love myself and the world equally.
The world does not mean more than me.
I spread love but, I must love myself first.

I'm open, like a book ready to be read.
I'm ready for the miracles in store for me.

I'm beyond proud of who I've become.
My mindset has evolved.
My priorities have aligned.
My tolerance has been re-invented.

My vibrations are magnetic.
I attract love.
I attract growth.
I attract abundance.
I attract everything I need.

I forgive those who have hurt me.
I forgive, not because they deserve it.
I forgive, for myself, *because I deserve it.*

I have more than enough on my plate.
I do not have to carry the burdens of others.

No one can bring me down.
My confidence whispers.
Their insecurities scream.

My boundaries should always be respected.
I deserve someone who is good for my mental health.

I will no longer be a people pleaser.
I will no longer give in to conformity.
I will not worry about who likes me.
I must like me.

I breathe free of toxic speech.
I let go of feeling inferior within myself.
I am worth more than what I may believe.

I have no space for hate.
I have no energy for anger.
I do not need negativity.
My aura is a temple.

I owe the beauty of success to myself.
I will do everything I set out to do.

It's okay if I only exist today.
I deserve to take a me day.
I deserve to rest.

Write your customized affirmations!

■

■

■

■

■

■

Write your customized affirmations!

-

-

-

-

-

Write your customized affirmations!

■

■

■

■

■

■

Write your customized affirmations!

■

■

■

■

■

A Note to You:

One day,
I hope when you walk past a mirror.
You love the person staring back at you.
And you will.
Please promise me that you will.

With love, Hope Moore.

Thank you for reading. I hope you enjoyed this collection, just as much as I loved writing it for you.

Tag me on Instagram @byhopemoore with pictures of your written affirmations for a chance to be featured on my page!

To stay up to date with all my future projects, including the "Tidal Waves" series: follow my Instagram @byhopemoore.

To buy merchandise, including canvases, and apparel visit my website: www.byhopemoore.com!

My poetry collection "Wilted Roses Unraveled" is on Amazon and Barnes and Noble.

Stay happy, continue healing, and keep falling in love with yourself!

Sincerely,
The Author,
Hope Moore.

Printed in Great Britain
by Amazon

76726493R00081